TEN Secrets to
GETTING
PROMOTED

TEN Secrets to GETTING PROMOTED

Carolyn Thompson

Ten Secrets to Getting Promoted

Everyone wants to get promoted. Being recognized for hard work and accomplishments makes one feel spectacular. You can't wait to share the good news with anyone and everyone who will listen.

While getting promoted makes you feel fantastic, being passed over for promotion can be devastating, so much so that you might consider leaving a particular company. There's nothing worse than feeling unappreciated — or in being passed over for a promotion, having another co-worker receive it, and finding that they are now your boss. Having your lunchtime confidante become your supervisor is one of the most difficult work-related situations anyone can face.

Having been an executive recruiter and career coach for over two decades, I've heard thousands of stories from people wanting to leave their positions because they weren't getting promoted. Yet, when discussing what benefits a company offers to make it an attractive place to work, human resources managers repeatedly endorse opportunities for promotion as a benefit to potential employees.

Everyone knows the most valuable resource to any company is the human capital, so why weren't these companies doing everything within their power to retain and promote as many people as possible?

Time and again it turns out that, rather than being the result of unfair company practice, the employees in question hadn't necessarily set themselves up for promotion.

Most of the problems that people experience in a job — whether with opportunities for advancement or in other areas — revolve around communications issues.

Having professional disagreements at work is really a matter of individuals expressing differing opinions. Many people don't speak up for themselves properly, or, vice versa, they overspeak for themselves, saying or doing things they wish they could take back.

Learning to properly handle conflict early on, gives you a better perspective when you find yourself in a difficult situation. People often make emotional choices when faced with conflict, rather than staying focused on using good business judgment and maintaining a big-picture perspective.

If some of these people had better planned their career trajectory they wouldn't have been passed over for promotion, leaving them feeling compelled to leave. If they'd thought things through and not reacted emotionally to business situations they encountered, they could have avoided some key conflicts that left others questioning their abilities. By the time I met them, they'd created reputations for themselves they were unable to reverse. Their promotability potential had already been damaged beyond repair.

My own career is instructive. I too was an employee who had been promoted as well as passed over for promotions in the past. I'd put in overtime, I'd exceeded my sales targets, and I'd tried hard to be a team player. Why didn't they promote me every time the opportunity presented itself? In seeking answers to this question, I discovered a wealth of information, some of it gleaned from corporate executives from across the country – a select group of respected individuals who have not only been promoted themselves quite often, but who have promoted others within their respective institutions.

I wanted to be able to share their insights, using them to answer a range of questions:

- **What makes some people more promotable than others, even though they are equally qualified?**

- **Why do some people repeatedly get passed over for promotion?**

- **What can someone do to ensure they get promoted and set themselves on a positive career trajectory from the beginning, learning to avoid the obvious pitfalls from the start?**

The executives I spoke with came from multiple disciplines and had insightful, career-building advice to share about promotions. In each interview, we discussed what makes someone promotable. Their responses were varied but, inevitably, they identified a number of essential personal attributes when considering an employee for promotion. Across the board, all the executives agreed: a good first impression is not enough. In order to create a path to promotion for yourself, you need to continuously exemplify traits of someone that represents the company well both inside and outside of work. You can't just be on your best behavior for a week or a month; you need to repeatedly exhibit your core beliefs through your actions. Demonstrable integrity, sustained over time, indicates you're promotable, someone who deserves recognition and can assume more responsibility.

Most of the attributes the executives look for are not things that can be faked:

- **Work ethic**

- **Honesty**

- **Dependability and reliability**

- **Poise, or grace**

- **Pride in your work**

- **Empathy for others**

- **Boldness in asking questions**

- **Ability to make decisions**

These qualities are all subjective, not objective, and are not simply achieved by exceeding quotas or being on time every day. You have to continue to maintain a consistently positive impression over time for everyone you work with.

I hope the advice contained in this book will help you apprehend and emulate the attributes that employers value; instead of waiting around for the next promotion, you'll create a promotion opportunity for yourself that is based upon honest recognition of your achievements.

Promotion is a privilege, not a right.

— George Rau, Executive Vice President of Human Resources

❋❋❋❋❋❋❋❋❋

ONE:

Lay low and observe for the first few months.

In most companies, you need to have gone through a full year's business cycle in order to better predict how things will play out year to year. You can learn a lot in a year: about the business, the culture, the competition, your boss' style, your coworkers. Your impression and performance in the first six months will determine your success for the duration of your employment at this company. With only one chance to make a first impression, it's a good idea to blend in with the group and stay low under the radar when possible, rather than have the spotlight focused on yourself, until you have a better understanding of the playing field. Be a sponge; soak up everything you can.

■ **Check your ego at the door.**

Whether you are a seasoned executive with a strong reputation as a change agent, or a hot shot academically accredited research scientist, it is difficult to change someone's first impression. If they meet your ego before they meet you, you're setting yourself up for disaster. Better to be recognized later for your accomplishments within the organization than to boast about your previous achievements so "they have some idea who they are dealing with." Let your past be your past and let your present guide your future, and let your actions speak for themselves.

Knowledge is power.

The more knowledge you have, the better decisions you will make, the more insightful your participation in group activities will be, and the better the impression you will create. You want to be the person others are coming to in order to brainstorm and discuss ideas, not the one constantly seeking out others for assistance.

It's a two-way street with supporting your coworkers; be available when someone shows up at your cubicle or door needing your help. If you're busy, set a time to get together that will work for both where you can dedicate uninterrupted time and focus on how you can be of assistance.

Study the lay of the land.

Examine those who are getting promoted in your organization and find out how they got there. Think about how to make their scenarios work for you. You may see a group or division where the team is very close, and when it comes time to identify a new manager for that group, the company decides to go outside. Why? The people seem well liked, and smart — what has occurred in that group that you want to avoid?

Perhaps as you start to think further about the group, you notice that all the people have the same set of skills and are at the same level. None of the players involved have a particular depth or breadth of experience that sets one apart from the other. Furthermore, they have limited exposure since they have all worked at only one or two companies in their careers (which can be limiting from a best practices standpoint). Sometimes, the company chooses to bring in a new manager from another company simply to gain the intellectual capital that person has accumulated by working in another environment. They've received different training, seen good and bad decisions made elsewhere and, while on the surface it may not seem fair to the people in the department, ultimately the company executives may benefit from information they learn from this new manager.

We all know it is in the company's best interest to promote you. You have knowledge that can't be relearned by hiring someone else. Make sure when given the chance to cross train or work with different individuals within the organization that you take that opportunity. Be mindful of the social landscape and how it changes from department to department.

Some managers are historically difficult to work with. I've learned that nine times out of ten it's because they have high expectations which have rarely been met. If you're ever faced with working for an overly demanding manager, be open and ask about his or her expectations so you can determine if you're possibly the exception to the rule and one of the few people that could make the cut. Many times, you can learn more from a challenging manager than you can from an easy-to-please one. Even if what you take away is how you don't want to manage people in the future, you have still learned a great deal you can apply later.

▨ Two ears, one mouth.

Many people will tell you they are great listeners. These people are generally the ones that talk more than they listen. You can learn a lot from people by listening, namely whether they are thinkers or feelers.

For example, after working all day on a complex PowerPoint presentation that is fundamentally completed, one person may remark:

"I <u>feel</u> this is ready to go."

Someone else on the team may express the same sentiment by saying:

"I <u>think</u> this is ready to go."

This is the difference between a thinker and a feeler. Every single person you interact with will send you signals of <u>thinking</u> and <u>feeling</u>. If you're able to isolate who in your work groups are thinkers or feelers, you create an immediate opportunity to connect with them in a fundamental way by communicating with them in their language. Try it...it works with personal relationships too. You'll find traditional barriers to understanding are instantly broken, enabling you to build associations more quickly.

▨ **Show, don't tell.**

Fiction writers know what I'm talking about here. Think about your favorite novels. The characters exhibit personal traits through their interactions with others which creates the image we have of them, positive or negative.

What impression, or character traits, do you want to leave with people? By identifying how you want others to perceive you, you can single out a few behaviors to consistently exemplify those qualities.

For example, if you want people to perceive you as hardworking, reliable, and dependable, you can be on time to work every day, refuse to call in sick, and offer to stay late to work on projects. You don't have to tell them, you can show them.

If you want people to perceive you as a knowledge leader, or a decisive person capable of being in charge, take a leadership role on a tough project and see it through to completion. You need to be organized, build consensus, handle conflict professionally, and take ownership and responsibility without being bossy. See something that's not right or that needs to be changed? Professionally approach management privately with solutions, not just complaints. If you can do these things, you'll never have to tell anyone how competent you are, they'll have witnessed it for themselves firsthand.

Think about people who have been successful on reality competition television shows. Individuals always emerge as the strong leaders by being decisive without being divisive. They gain consensus, thereby outing the nonbe-lievers, and they build empathy and synergy within the group by maximizing people's strengths, downplaying their weaknesses, allowing people to take responsibility for their part of a task, and thereby earning their own recognition for a job well done.

You can't get called up to play in the game if you're not wearing the uniform.

— Holly Wittenberg, MBA

✦✦✦✦✦✦✦✦✦

TWO:
Dress for success.

In today's professionally casual work environment, it is important not be too casual. All promotable people put forth a professional image at all times. Even when the occasion calls for casual attire, they are well groomed and pressed without being overdressed. How do they do it? In some cases less is more; in this case more is less. More effort put up front means less gossip behind your back. If you want people to view you professionally, you need to project professionalism.

Sure, it's OK to have a fun time dressing, showing some individuality, but you don't want to be the one shown as "Glamour Don't" in the company newsletter.

Conform to what the company standards are. You'll want to follow the lead of what managers and supervisors are wearing to be promoted.

If you're not sure of the impression you're making, look around you — at the airport, the mall, at lunch, or a party. Who stands out as poised, confident, and professional? Look at their shoes, their accessories, and their haircuts. Clothing is a great conversation starter and most people are flattered if you ask them politely where they bought their shirt or shoes. You can consult a professional at a department store in the tailored clothing or personal shopping area. Their services are free and you are not obligated to buy anything, but they are often experts about fit, cut, and quality.

Hair, nails, and personal grooming are immediate silent statements of your personality. Tattoos and piercings are also outward expressions of your individuality and, if you're trying to get promoted at work, you might want to consider not showing them off in the office.

■ Women:

In a professional environment, showing too much skin on the top or the bottom will likely not work in your favor when it comes time to be promoted. You also don't need to spend thousands of dollars to be considered well dressed.

Make sure your clothes fit well first. The clothes you wear affect the way you feel from the inside out. If your skirt or pants are too tight, you're not fooling anyone by covering it up or keeping the jacket buttoned. Unfortunately, a poorly fitting suit is distracting and the impression you subconsciously pass on is that you're uncomfortable. Even if it means purchasing a larger size and having it tailored to properly fit, you will project a more positive self image if your clothes are comfortable. You'll actually look thinner if they fit you well.

Be mindful of trends that come and go if you are building a wardrobe for future success. Well-constructed blazers and jackets will never go out of style in fabrics that stand the test of time. Look for conservative patterns or solids that you can pair with patterns and that are constructed of fabrics that travel well such as gabardine, twill, silk blends, or wool for winter. Linens tend to fade and stain over time, so consider the long-term investment, as well as the shape and climate where you live and/or work.

Accessories are important, particularly shoes, handbags, and/or portfolios. Conservative is always better: minimize jewelry, particularly if it makes noise when you move, like a charm bracelet. Your shoes should be shined, the heel taps should not show nails through the bottom…if they do, have them repaired for just a few dollars. Your hand-bag should not be overflowing with Price Club receipts, baby bottles, granola bars, vitamin packs, etc. Keep your business cards handy at all times in a card case so they are not stained when you hand them out.

Makeup should always be professional, not dramatic, and don't overdo the perfume.

■ Men:

Pay attention to the details, particularly how your clothes fit. Your pants should have a slight crease, called a break, above your shoes and below your knees. If they don't they are too short. Wearing properly fitting and tailored pants, even if they are casual, shows that you care about your appearance. Your shirts should be well pressed and not fraying or discolored at the collar or sleeve.

Go through your closet once a year and select those clothes that aren't quite shipshape and donate them to charity. Take the chance to help others with their climb up the ladder (and get a tax deduction for your charitable donation!). Continue to invest in your wardrobe.

Excessive jewelry and cologne are not necessary to be considered for promotion.

Personal Internet appearance.

Nearly every person is "Google-searched" before coming on board and regularly after being hired. Make sure your LinkedIn, Facebook, Twitter, and other Web presences you maintain are professional and portray you in a light that shows you are ready to be promoted.

Be prepared.

When faced with meetings, make sure you are on time and prepared. You don't want to overrun the room with your own personal agenda, but bring a notepad, a pen, your completed presentation or talking points. And smile. Say hello to everyone and introduce yourself to those you haven't met when time allows.

No matter what's going on in your personal life, leave it outside the office. Personal chitchat should always be kept light and positive. Focus on the work.

Be friendly with everyone but don't make your friends at work.

— Greg Brown, CEO

✦✦✦✦✦✦✦✦✦✦

THREE:

Conduct yourself professionally.

Over 50 percent of the reasons people are let go or passed over for promotion fall under the areas of professional conduct, or lack thereof. This is a diverse topic and these are easy traps to fall into so be aware!

■ **Don't use the company computer or phones for personal reasons.**

Even if you are having lunch at your desk, be mindful of what's on your screen or the conversations you are having with your friends and family. Unless it's required for your job, don't read the paper or magazines at your desk or online; it's best to read for personal reasons offsite. If you find yourself perusing a newspaper while consuming a quick sandwich over the noon hour, it's advisable to do so with your feet under your desk as opposed to on top. Consider shutting your door if you have an office in case those passing by don't recognize that you are on your lunch break.

Lunchtime is great networking time — even if you're bringing in Lean Cuisine or brown-bagging it. Even if no one else is eating in the lunchroom, give it a try. Before you know it, you'll have met a couple of new people each week. You never know where that personal connection might lead in the future.

▨   Be on time. Don't call in sick unless you are very ill.

A lot of people misuse sick time for personal errands. A little planning ahead can pay big dividends when it comes time for promotion. Set aside one personal day every other month, or once a quarter, to catch up on doctor appointments, home deliveries, and repairs. This enables you to budget your time appropriately so when it comes time to schedule your regular appointments, you know in advance what day works for you.

Of course, kids get sick and pipes burst without notice so do your best to practice as much preventative mainte-nance as possible to minimize last-minute life crises that might interfere with your work schedule. If you find your-self calling in sick or needing to take the day off unexpect-edly once a week, or even once a month, you may need to consider finding some outside assistance with the events that are causing you to miss work. Maybe that's a daytime babysitter, friend, or neighbor who can help out; perhaps it is finding repair people that you can trust to work without your direct supervision.

▨   Request time off in advance and not during busy times of the year.

Many companies have guidelines regarding vacation and leave time, so try to plan ahead. If you know you want to go skiing over the holidays you may want to request time off well in advance, as many people request time off at the holidays. If you know your project has a deliverable and you're getting married, you might want to consider planning the wedding for a month after the deliverable so you can really enjoy such a momentous occasion with your family and friends and truly relax during your honeymoon.

If you have family obligations, be up front about them but don't make demands.

Work one-on-one with your supervisor to discuss personal needs that affect your work schedule. Your supervisor is much more likely to work with you individually if you ask for consideration but don't demand it as a condition of employment. Remember, they are paying you to do a job and you need to deliver. Balancing your kid's soccer tournaments, your aging parents' needs, or other requirements with your work demands will make you more organized and show people that you can handle responsibility without getting flustered.

Be social, but stay out of office gossip.

Whether you're invited to lunch with a group of people or over to someone's house for a weekend barbecue, you need to make time to get to know your coworkers on a personal level. Show genuine interest, but be mindful of the line between colleague and personal friend.

Should a conversation take a turn toward gossip, whether in or outside of the office, try to remain neutral. Not commenting one way or the other is easily accomplished by saying, "I really don't know them that well to comment." You also may be put in a situation where you feel compelled to defend someone else. Calmly pointing out their position in the situation, without emotion, can be communicated with something like, "It's possible their intention was..." or "Perhaps they were thinking..." Both of these statements are very different from, "Well she told me..." or "He said that the reason he did that was..."

Gossip is very destructive and, I promise you, if someone is gossiping about another person, he or she is gossiping about you too, so try to avoid putting yourself out there as a topic for other people's conversations.

■ **Limit your alcohol intake.**

When attending evening or weekend functions don't stay too late and always conduct yourself with personal integrity. Eat something before you go so you won't be starved and, if alcohol is served, you don't want to overdo it. The easiest way to control your alcohol intake at a work function is to have a glass of water between each drink. This ensures you have a glass in your hand but significantly lowers your alcohol intake if you feel the need to have a drink.

Conversations with coworkers outside the office can quickly spin out of control or get too personal. Don't fool yourself into thinking those comments everyone thought were hilarious over drinks on Saturday won't make it back to the office Monday morning. If you feel the topic veering off course, politely excuse yourself and move to another conversation group at the gathering.

Gossip seems most rampant when companies go through significant change—during mergers, acquisitions, layoffs, executive changes—employees are compelled to discuss the situation among themselves. Again, try to do your best to remain neutral, and refocus on the work at hand. Even if you are feeling uncertain or might agree with what's being said, if you don't say anything it can never come back to haunt you.

Be proactive, not reactive.

Think ahead and forge relationships built on trust. If someone does something that really irritates you, think about how you can move forward without reacting to the situation. Even if you feel the need to give someone a piece of friendly advice, unless the person asked you for it, your advice is strictly your opinion and you'll best serve your own interests keeping it to yourself.

People are the priority, not the device.

Don't make your BlackBerry the priority; the person in front of you is more important to communicate with than someone in cyberspace. The most successful CEOs turn off their PDAs when they are in meetings. They give the person in front of them their full time and attention.

■ **Wait twenty-four hours to send an angry or potentially controversial e-mail.**

Once you type something—and push send—you can't take it back. Consider scheduling a one-on-one private conversation <u>after</u> you've taken time to cool off rather than sending an e-mail that may be misinterpreted or perpetuate the disagreement further. Many times people have personal things going on that affect their judgment and reactions at work. Don't rush to criticize someone, or so fiercely defend your position that it causes a rift with a coworker or supervisor. Take a day, really think about why you are so upset, and determine if this is a battle that you want to fight.

Remember, we can't change other people; we can only control how we react to them. By keeping your cool and evaluating the importance of the situation rather than reacting emotionally, you'll impress people as someone that doesn't crack under pressure.

Pursue your passion.

–Barry Mumford, Senior Director

●●●●●●●●●●

FOUR:
Know your value proposition from both sides.

The key to knowing why you want to be promoted is to be honest with yourself about both what you want and what you offer. Many people want to be promoted because of the increased pay, or perceived increased authority—and status. Ultimately there has to be something in it for the company as well.

So ask yourself:

■ **Is it a title you are looking for or more responsibility?**

Sometimes a lateral move will enhance skills that you need to ultimately accept more responsibility. Is it that you're ready for the challenge or that you're looking for outward validation of your expertise?

■ **Are you bored with your work?**

Know what you enjoy doing and where your strengths are to maximize your potential. Surround yourself with others that complement your weaknesses with their strengths and learn from them so you can enhance areas of weakness. Increasing your breadth and depth of experience also provides challenge if you're feeling you've mastered your responsibilities.

Focusing on your weaknesses can also lead to unexpected feelings of inadequacy, so be prepared! If you start trying to do things you're not familiar with, or are not good at, it is possible to master them, but at what cost? Remember, everyone has strengths and weaknesses and we can't all be good at everything. While you should do your best to learn new things, if you find yourself losing self-confidence because the learning curve is very steep, be happy with giving it a try. Recognizing your weakness is a huge accomplishment in itself and enables you to appreciate that quality or skill in others.

▧ Do you just want a raise?

Your boss will not give you a raise because you bought a larger house, got a new car, or expanded your family. Don't just barge into your boss' office one day because you're stressed out about money, shut the door, plop yourself in the chair across the desk, and tell him or her about all your personal reasons for needing more money.

Take the opportunity to discuss your compensation at your annual review or set a private appointment to ask for a raise. Increased pay is awarded because it's earned by your performance. It is simply not dictated by your personal financial situation.

Learning to ask for a raise is an art in itself. The key is to justify your position by compiling a measurable list of accomplishments and contributions. This could include growth in profit or sales, or reduction in expenses or costs directly associated with your work. Even if your company is struggling financially, if you are outperforming your peers, you'll want to have a compelling list of justifications for your request.

Do you think your boss has it in for you and will never give you what you want?

It's possible, but in general, people are not calculating and malicious, although we are often paranoid and anxious. Maybe it's your approach. Focus on what's in it for them, not what's in it for you. Doing so will give you the content to focus on in your conversation to justify your request—whether you are asking for an increase in pay, title, or responsibility.

Work outside your job title.

–Don Neff, Chief Financial Officer

●●●●●●●●●

FIVE:

Align yourself with others who are getting promoted.

If you want the boss' job, make his or her job easier. Go above and beyond what's asked and expected of you. Internal and external networking are equally important. Keeping your pulse on what's hot in your industry keeps you current and relevant and gives you plenty to talk about when you need to.

■ **Raise your hand to volunteer on projects.**

There are lots of projects that go on at any company where you can become involved by simply raising your hand. Whether that's organizing the company's softball team and ordering uniforms, working on a tedious inventory project, assisting with the holiday party, or taking on a hard-to-please client, these things get you noticed, particularly when they are well executed.

Make sure you're not overextending yourself between work and personal commitments, but create opportunities to interact with others at your company. It could be Web site redesign, a company move, or even a computer system conversion or integration. The more people you meet and favorably impress, the better liked and trusted you'll become.

■ **Ask people to grab a coffee or a sandwich.**

People who are being promoted are busy. You want to get five minutes to pick their brains whenever possible and an easy way to do this is to bring them lunch. They'll appreciate the gesture and likely share sage advice or pertinent information that will benefit you. You don't want to be an obvious brownnoser, but carving time out for yourself on successful people's calendars can be a valuable self-investment when promotion time comes around. Having shared a lunch or two can go along way when an impromptu brainstorming session occurs between managers discussing their direct reports and their future potential.

■ **Be genuine in your interaction and desire to get to know people on a professional level.**

People can smell a rat a mile away. If you spend all of your time scheming, it will be obvious and damage your relationships with both your peers and your managers. Treat everyone with the same respect, spending equal time getting to know your coworkers as well as managers and subordinates. It takes a team of people to make each other successful and you can build valuable relationships throughout the organization so that when you are promoted you'll know who can—and can't—be counted on.

▓ **Improve your communications skills.**

Text messaging and e-mail have infiltrated organizations— so much so, that often verbal communication is lacking. If you haven't had the opportunity to do presentations in person, join a local Toastmasters group. (www.toast-masters.org). You'll meet people from all walks of life and have the chance to hone your skills in a constructive environment.

If you speak English as a second language, this is particularly crucial for your future promotion. You need to speak clearly, using proper grammar and selecting proper verb tenses. Practice will build your confidence when speaking in front of groups, knowing that you are well spoken and easily understood.

How many times have you sent an e-mail and your intention was misunderstood? If you had a personal conversation discussing the same topic, your tone and intonation may have better directed the conversation. But in e-mail, all you do is type your words to be personally interpreted by the receiver. It's one-way communication. A good rule of thumb is to keep e-mails to three sentences. If it takes more than four sentences, you may want to have a conversation first, and then reiterate the salient points in a follow-up e-mail.

It's always better to communicate directly than to have your writing misinterpreted. And vice versa—if you receive e-mails that you perceive as cold or rude, don't overthink things. Instead, pick up the phone and talk through the issues at hand directly with the person. You'll find middle ground sooner and get more accomplished faster in a conversation. Follow up afterward with an e-mail containing salient points without emotion or opinions to misconstrue.

People for whom English is a second language are most often passed over for promotion because of poor communication skills. To improve your writing skills enroll in a local creative writing group or college-level writing course. Practice makes perfect and other than writing e-mails and presentations for work, few people practice their writing outside of work. E-mail leaves a lasting impression on people, particularly supervisors. If you cannot communicate clearly and concisely in writing, you will be passed over for promotion.

▨ Attend continuing education classes, conferences, and networking events specific to your work/ industry at least twice a year.

Keeping current on topics pertaining to your industry ensures you will be able to anticipate trends that may affect your promotability. In our most recent recession, many people, particularly in manufacturing, had problems not only getting promoted but finding new jobs. This didn't happen overnight. Outsourcing of manufacturing jobs to other countries and the increase of imported goods have made a lot of these jobs in the United States obsolete. Many of these people have transferrable skills and could have easily made a jump to other industries when unemployment was low. As unemployment rises, jobs become scarcer; employers become more selective, thereby creating a surplus of people in an industry where there are fewer jobs. Should you find yourself in a career path where you see jobs dwindling rather than being increased, consider where else you might be able to apply your skills and expertise. Industry conferences are great places to get ideas of what types of new opportunities are on the rise.

Progress occurs when courageous, skillful leaders seize the opportunity to change things for the better.

–Harry S. Truman

●●●●●●●●●●

SIX:
Discuss advancement opportunities with your supervisor at your review.

▪ **Ask, don't demand.**

Celebrating an anniversary at the company doesn't entitle you to a promotion. If your boss doesn't offer you a promotion, take time at your annual review to ask for specific clarification of what his or her expectations are in order that you can be promoted. Be clear, and document the targets in writing for future reference. It's possible you may get a new boss within the next twelve months. Writing down the targets creates a paper trail and will alleviate the need to start all over from scratch. Moreover, it will open the door to discuss what the expectations are in order to stay on track for a promotion.

Having met and exceeded your established targets, being on time, and a well-rounded, engaged employee generally qualifies someone for promotion; however, your perception of your performance may be different than your supervisor's. And remember, it's his or her perception that counts when it comes time for review.

Use any criticism constructively.

Even if you don't agree when someone tells you something, the person is telling you what his or her impression or perception is. Whether it was something you said, or did, you led the person to that conclusion. If there was a misunderstanding, take time to discuss it, but don't immediately go on the defensive.

When you feel the need to defend yourself over an issue, apply these common conflict resolution tactics to your advantage. Recognize the other person's viewpoint, clarifying his or her position. No matter how hard it is, you will avoid conflict if you find common ground with the person, and offer positive steps for the future instead of defending the past. No matter how strongly you disagree with someone's perception of your past decisions or performance, it is in the past, and it is his or her opinion. It's unlikely you will be able to change it and taking a defensive posture creates the opening for heightened conflict. Consciously disengaging yourself from the conflict moves your conversation and relationship forward with a proactive approach to the future.

It's unlikely you will ever win a heated argument with your boss. You'll only damage the future relationship. Take the criticism and move forward, knowing that whatever the situation was you want to avoid it in the future, and likely will if you're attentive.

■ **Be keenly aware of what openings there are and apply selectively to them with your supervisor's approval.**

I placed a person with a Fortune 100 company who was promoted nine times over his first seven years with the company, nearly tripling his starting salary. Ultimately, he left the company after fifteen years, and he'd been promoted twelve times. I've never known anyone who better mastered the internal move than he. When I asked him about his strategy, he told me as soon as he settled into a new position, he networked up so that when the next opportunity came about, the decision makers always knew his background qualifications and how he could make an immediate positive impact. When he wasn't personally tapped for certain jobs, he asked for them, using his value proposition to make it nearly impossible for them not to choose him.

I remember the day when he told me he competed for a job against the manager who had originally hired him, and he won the job, despite having less overall experience. He had a plan, and he executed it well.

Applying for any and/or every job that opens up will become annoying to your supervisors as well as human resources. Apply selectively, with your supervisor's endorsement, and know your personal value proposition.

Consider the impact working from home will have on both your personal life and career path.

–Lisa Cines, Managing Partner

■■■■■■■◉◉◉

SEVEN:
Work from home only when approved and necessary.

Working from home removes you from the day-to-day and you can be forgotten even if you are doing a great job. While it's a great perk, it can get in the way of being noticed.

Technology is amazing and you can use it to your advantage if working from home is pulling you out of the lunchtime crowd. Web conferencing, using SKYPE or other methods of visual contact, will enable you to have a closer connection to people you work with remotely.

If you have the opportunity to work from home, use it with discretion. Many last-minute decisions are made on a daily basis in the office and you might be overlooked if you're not making yourself available and noticed in the workplace.

Working from home is great to avoid commuting time and to maximize work / life balance, as long as you don't let your home work environment distract you. Set up a separate work space where you can concentrate without interruption, take calls, and focus on your assignments.

Your supervisor can see how productive you are, even from home. Whether that's a report you submit or one that is automatically generated by your computer, your productivity is being measured. BlackBerry time is not generally considered productive time; although it is an excellent way to monitor your e-mail away from your computer. So be mindful of what your job requires and how you're allocating your work-from-home time.

*Don't go around saying the world owes you a living;
the world owes you nothing; it was here first.*

–Mark Twain

EIGHT:
Don't openly complain.

No matter the offenses, never openly complain about your job, your pay, your boss, or your company.

Everyone has good and bad days. Even your boss. But just as you don't want to hear others complaining about things, don't be the one leading the charge if you're unhappy. Trying to create sympathy for your misery is the quickest way to put a target on your back should layoffs come down the pike.

Take a day off to really think about it.

Is it really that bad that you can't work through it? The grass isn't always greener, so think long and hard about your situation. Can you make a subtle change in how you do things or conduct yourself to make the situation better?

One of the principles of anger management says that we can't change those things (or people) that make us mad; we can only change how we react to them. Is it possible to look at the situation from another's point of view and see another side?

▨ **If you aren't happy with something, follow the proper channels in a positive manner.**

If you escalate something properly and with quiet discretion, you'll likely get a resolution one way or the other. There's nothing more frustrating than feeling like no one's listening to you. But even if the CEO has an open-door policy, you shouldn't demand time on his or her calendar to air your personal grievances if you haven't first followed the proper channels with human resources and/or your direct manager.

Give them adequate time to respond and ask for timelines in which you can expect a response. Large companies often move slowly, so be patient, yet persistent. It's also important to be ready to accept that the resolution might not be what you anticipated. Even when things don't go the way we want them to, we can always respond professionally.

▨ **Treat everyone with respect despite what you might really think about them.**

Keeping your opinions private is important when you feel yourself becoming judgmental about someone at work. Holding your thoughts in check will ensure you don't say something you might regret later.

There's nothing attractive about bullies in grade school and they generally grow up to become bullies at work. It's easy to join in when someone's being singled out or made fun of, but avoiding it and being kind to that person will pay off in the end.

▦ Don't ask others about pay.

Others may ask you, though, even if you don't ask them. When confronted with this situation it can be uncomfortable. One professional way to respond would be, "Oh, I'm sorry, I'm just not comfortable discussing my finances at work. It's nothing personal." If the person keeps pushing, be firm. Remember, knowledge is power and once you discuss pay, the other person has power over you.

Discussion of salary almost always comes about when someone resigns to go to a new job. It's inevitable that someone will ask, "How much money did you get?" I'm here to tell you, no matter how well you know people or how close you are, 90 percent of the time they inflate the number they tell their friends. Don't believe everything you hear. Companies have pretty strict guidelines regarding compensation and benefits. If it sounds too good to be true it probably is. Most companies in a geographic area pay equally for similar jobs.

▦ Avoid airing your grievances on the Internet.

Your Facebook page, personal blog, or complaint Web sites are other places you should not publicly air your workplace displeasure. Even though you may think no one from your company is on your friend list it's easy to view people's wall posts. Steer clear of Web sites like JobVent.com where people complain about their companies, bosses, etc. Again, you never know who is reading these posts and, although it may seem anonymous, if you read between the lines your boss or coworker may be able to find out that it's you who is posting complaints.

■ **Work / life balance comes from within. It is not a benefit from your company.**

This goes back to planning and organization. We all have personal lives to juggle, no matter what our level. Whether your job is to work at the reception desk, the mail room, or the executive office, we have personal and professional responsibilities to everyone around us.

Accurate scheduling can help. Scheduling 75 percent of your time to allow for distractions is a great rule of thumb. Keeping one calendar that has work and personal commitments on it enables you not to double book yourself. When you under commit and over deliver, you'll leave people wanting more. Handling your personal life in conjunction with your professional responsibilities will ensure a path to promotion. When was the last time that someone who couldn't get to work on time, who called in sick or missed meetings was the person that got the promotion?

Accepting criticism constructively and asking what qualities, experience, or skill sets are necessary to be promoted is more effective than demands or ultimatums.

–Jenna Fiorito, Vice President

●●●●●●●●●●

NINE:
Don't be disappointed if you don't get the first promotion.

Even though you've worked hard, you've played by the rules, and you feel ready to be promoted, you might not be selected. I know I thought I was ready so many times in the past, and my boss just didn't seem to see it the same way. Now, with the wisdom that comes with time, I can see that I didn't have necessary knowledge or experience that the job required to be successful. With promotion comes heightened expectations; sometimes, you just need to have some experience under your belt to meet those expectations. It would be worse, in the long run, to be promoted to a position you couldn't be successful at.

The example we discussed earlier where the company wants to gain some expertise from a competitor or related company so they bring someone in from outside is pertinent here. Sometimes the company brings in fresh blood in the form of a new manager from a competitor or another industry to get a fresh perspective. You can't always compete with that need.

When companies go through mergers and acquisitions, part of the process is eliminating duplicate positions, so people will be let go to create efficiencies. If this happens to a supervisor that you have a great relationship with, don't panic. You may feel sad that your relationship is changing, but you should remain optimistic that your new supervisor will offer you something great as well. It's possible you may be getting the best boss you have ever had. It's also possible that the two of you might not see eye to eye and if that's the case, then you are now better equipped to handle it. No matter what the situation, the past professional relationship could lead to new opportunities in the future.

Your new boss may even be someone who was previously, or even recently, your coworker. This is probably the most difficult situation to be in, particularly when you applied for the job as well. When your confidant becomes your boss, your relationship changes—even if the exchanges between you don't seem to have changed, and you've had a great conversation about the situation. This person is now your boss, and ultimately the person who may hold your promotion fate in his or her hands.

While your inclination may be to run the other way, now more than ever it's important to have a clear-cut understanding of what you need to achieve in order to be considered for the next role opening up in your department, or to apply for a position in another department with his or her blessing. Requesting a meeting to set forth mutually clear expectations about your performance outside of the standard review process would be appropriate as soon as the person has settled into his or her new role.

No matter what the situation, being passed over for a promotion better equips you for a future position where you will be the one making the choices, giving out the good (or bad) news to the members of your team. If you haven't had the experience you can't understand how it feels. If you have had it happen you can speak from a direct position of experience and empathy.

It's not about you doing all the work; you are your people.

–Dan O'Donnell, Assistant Vice President

●●●●●●●●●●

TEN:

Be gracious when you get promoted.

You've made a monumental achievement! Be proud of yourself and celebrate your accomplishment with your family and friends outside of work.

■ **Bragging is not attractive.**

Modesty is an attractive trait in trustworthy people. Even though you may have clawed and scratched your way to that promotion, don't rub it in others' faces, particularly those who also applied for the job. Even as a joke, no one takes it as a joke and that can really come back to bite you.

■ **Set an example for those around you and treat them as you wanted and want to be treated.**

Lead by example; delegating wisely without micromanaging. Allowing for individuality is a great recipe for success. Settle into your new role being ever mindful that everyone around you is watching and taking notes. Your subordinates are trying to figure out how you got to where you are so they can replicate your path for themselves and your bosses are watching to make sure they made the right decision.

Continuing to conduct yourself with your next promotion in mind will help you with tough decisions and challenging situations that cross your path. Managing people is not easy; if your company doesn't offer full-fledged management training, and many don't, it's wise to seek some out on your own. There are many books on the subject but nothing takes the place of good old-fashioned exchange of ideas from people who've been there. Weekend workshops and retreats can be a great place to meet managers from other companies you can share things with confidentially and get some good advice.

Don't pull rank.

Just because you can, doesn't mean you should. If the answer to why you're doing something is because you can, you may be misusing your entitlement for your own ego. Keep it in check.

Think ahead.

You don't want this to be your last promotion, so don't get lazy. Keep up the good work, thinking about the future and how you're going to get there. You'll remain constantly challenged, and continuously well compensated.

If you make a mistake, alert your boss, and apologize—
don't cover it up. Accept responsibility for your actions
instead of trying to justify them. "I'm sorry"
is a very powerful statement.

—Fernando Gonzalez, Chief Financial Officer

◆◆◆◆◆◆◆◆◆◆

You're more likely to be promoted in an institution or company where you have a track record of success as opposed to being hired by a new employer into a position of greater responsibility and title than you have held previously. Even if you've made a few mistakes along the way. As long as you learn from your mistakes, apologize for them, and don't make the same mistake twice, chances are that your employer will recoup the investment in you and your success will continue to pay off. By giving you more responsibility, you will continue your ongoing commitment to bettering the company, its products, sales, etc.

What ifs?

■ **What if I made a major error and can't recover from it?**

It may be time to leave. You can often overcome one error but several may be more difficult. When you start at your new company, learn from your previous mistakes and leave your bad habits behind. Your new company is a chance to start with a clean slate. Go back to thinking about how you want to be perceived and start projecting yourself in that manner from the first day.

■ **What if I have applied several times and I'm not getting promoted?**

Have a one-on-one with your boss and ask exactly what you need to do to get ahead. If you complete the tasks and still aren't getting ahead, don't be bitter, but it may be time to prepare your resume to leave.

What if I'm on a probationary work plan and want to get out of my department but my boss won't approve it?

Very few companies will transfer someone on a performance improvement plan until they've completed it. Do your best to exceed their expectations, then look in other departments or other companies for new opportunities.

What if my friend and neighbor at another company insists that his or her company has a better higher-paying job for me?

Money isn't everything, but it never hurts to further investigate. If you're extended an opportunity to interview at another company on referral, you have a very high chance of getting an offer. Eighty percent of people get new jobs on referral; so when the chance comes, you should entertain it. Remember, there's no decision to be made unless they offer you the job, so don't jump ahead of yourself or the process and assume every interview will result in an offer. Just go in with an open mind and decide if the opportunity is interesting enough for you to pursue.

▨ What if my industry and/or company has deteriorated and positions are extremely competitive?

Identify your transferrable skills and personally network with people at companies hiring individuals with those skills. Be open to relocation on your dime to take advantage of jobs that might be offered to you in other parts of the country. Unemployment and labor demands vary widely so do your research and you'll find a new job.

▨ What if I'm just ready to leave?

Conduct a discreet, personal job search and leave on a professional note—leave a positive impression and never burn bridges. You can't predict where people are going to end up, so on your exit interview, while its tempting to try to sink that manager that made your life miserable, the negativity you put out will ultimately come back to haunt you. If you can articulate your thoughts in a constructive manner, do so, but if you can't, it is you who will look bad, not others, no matter how bad they are.

TEN SECRETS TO GETTING PROMOTED

1. Lay low and observe for the first few months.

2. Dress for success.

3. Conduct yourself professionally.

4. Know your value proposition from both sides.

5. Align yourself with others who are getting promoted.

6. Discuss advancement opportunities with your supervisor at your review.

7. Work from home only when approved and necessary.

8. Don't openly complain.

9. Don't be disappointed if you don't get the first promotion.

10. Be gracious when you get promoted.

Acknowledgements

I owe numerous debts of gratitude to many people for their support and encouragement over the years. In particular I'd like to thank those people directly involved with the publication of this book:

My loving husband, James, for being a constant source of support and an excellent proofreader.

My immediate family and friends for their encouragement and feedback. For those family, friends, and colleagues no longer with us: you are missed but never forgotten.

Maria Frawley, PhD, and Gail Cato for being amazing editors. Your input was invaluable.

My Pinnacle Society colleagues: I find inspiration in each of you and am grateful to you all for helping me find my voice.

All the candidates I have placed in the past as well as clients who have hired people from me. There are so many more people out there that I would like to help. I hope they will find my various publications helpful in their career planning.

My past and present coworkers, employees, coaching clients, and business partners: I appreciate all that you do and have done for me, particularly Lindsay Sellner—I don't know how I could get it all done without you.

Nicole LaFlamme—thanks for your thoughtful input. Your father and I are so proud of you!

Author Bio

Carolyn Thompson resides in the Washington, DC, area and has been an executive recruiter since 1988. Carolyn is a creative entrepreneur and a certified career coach. She is a frequent contributor to national news organizations such as MSNBC, CNN, NPR, *The Wall Street Journal* and *The Washington Post*. Her articles on career development and the employment industry have been published in various national magazines, trade journals, and on the Internet. A frequent speaker on the subjects of career development, recruiting, and motivation, she is a member of the Pinnacle Society* and the International Coach Federation.**

Carolyn is an alumnus of Kansas State University and author of *TEN EASY STEPS TO A PERFECT RESUME* and *TEN STEPS TO FINDING THE PERFECT JOB*, now available on Amazon.

Her Web site is **www.CarolynThompson.net** and you can find her blog at **www.JobSearchJungle.com**

www.pinnaclesociety.org
The Pinnacle Society is the nation's premier consortium of top recruiters within the permanent placement industry. Since 1989, membership is limited to seventy-five of the nation's top recruiters.

**www.coachfederation.org*
The International Coach Federation is the largest worldwide resource for business and personal coaches.